VEILED

NZONONYE GODSGLORY

~VEILED~

To my father; MR Nzononye Onyemaechi Emmanuel, and Uncle Christian for helping me discover this talent of mine.

Contents

POEMS

Foreword

~VEILED~

VEILED is an emotion raging collection of poetry which exposes love, betrayal, despair, sadness and melancholic nature of humans. It also gives an instinct of hustle and rejection. The book **VEILED** showcases several literary devices such as imagery, simile, personification, rhetorical question etc. The rhyming pattern is there to give easy flow of words.

Consider these few lines-

She hides her image

From this stage

(Veiled)

Take me with you

To a place where love interrupts

And peace erupts

With its fragrance falling like dew

(A Love I Crave)

Don't tell him I laid with you

The thought of it makes me ewe

(Adultery)

Single yet a parent

A mother of two

A father too

A burden so transparent

(Single Yet a Parent)

These are delicacies you just must not miss. You will find more as you read the entire collection.

Acknowledgements

~VEILED~

VEILED is an emotion raging collection of poetry which exposes love, betrayal, despair, sadness and melancholic nature of humans. It also gives an instinct of hustle and rejection. The book **VEILED** showcases several literary devices such as imagery, simile, personification, rhetorical question etc. The rhyming pattern is there to give easy flow of words.

Consider these few lines-

She hides her image

From this stage

(Veiled)

Take me with you

To a place where love interrupts

And peace erupts

With its fragrance falling like dew

(A Love I Crave)

Don't tell him I laid with you

The thought of it makes me ewe

(Adultery)

Single yet a parent

A mother of two

A father too

A burden so transparent

(Single Yet a Parent)

ACKNOWLEDGEMENTS

These are delicacies you just must not miss. You will find more as you read the entire collection.

Litany Of Poems

POEMS

POEMS

A Love ICrave

Take me with you

To a place where love interrupts

And peace erupts

With its fragrance falling like dew

To be engrossed in this feeling

Is all I want

A love so appealing

Is all I crave

Hold me with you

In the twilight's view

Dark as night that bares the naked moon

With an unending love tune

To be lost in thus mood

With the waves of wind dancing besides us

To share this priceless moment

Where love cannot be subdued.

Letter to My Ex

I hope you tell her

That I was once your lover

Though we didn't last

It's all in the past

The more I loved

The more you fled

And the less care I showed

The more we became untold

I hope you reminisce

Of our first kiss

It was a bliss

I truly miss

I wish you tell her

I came first

Boring her

With the memories of us

Give Me Life or Give Me Death

Give me life or give me death

That's all there is

For time is short

Make it count

Give me love or give me hate

For infatuation is fornication

And in lust I have dwelled

I lie not

Make me or mar me

For whosoever makes; loves

And whosoever mares is inhuman

Keep me or lose me

For I love whom I love

And despise whom I despise

Veiled

Her pains she hopes to manage

But her heart is damaged

She is cloned

By that face she wears

She is wounded

And abide in fears

She is full of scars

But hides from who we are

A glance closer

You would see clearer

The hurt she covers

…..she is broken

Yet she reins in her pains

Sweet Lies

Tongue wagging

Lips blushing

All to the words of the lips

Sweet lies

Intention concealed

Hidden motives

Just to gain your attention

Sweet lies

Words blasting out

Crushing the mind like arrows

But arrows filled with the fantasy

Of unimagined ecstasy

Smiling innocently but foolishly

To the lies of the

Wasting time meant to be priceless

Sweet lies.

Golden Memories

(A Tribute)

How I wish I could clone her

She left too soon

My love should have restrained her

Or perhaps, it wasn't strong enough

Even in death

Still and solid as rock can be

She's lain in mother earth

Embalmed with dust

Even in death

Cold and chill as ice can be

She's lain in mother earth

Responding to nature's call

Death could take all

But not my memories of you

Unrequited Love

My love was like a red rose

That sprung off beautifully

Hoping you caught a glimpse

Of what I intended

With strained scowls

She frowned at my intentions

Shattered are the words

That held much emotions

I have a hole in my heart

A pain I can't rip off

In the midnight of sorrow

I'm endlessly waiting for the morrow

Grasping tightly to my pillow

Since you've placed my love on detention

Knowing how much I craved its attention

I'd learn to live with this tension
knowing I had lost your affection

Broken

I watch him helplessly

As he cheats endlessly

My heart bleeds as it shatters

The sight of him with another

My voice is gone

From crying till dawn

Wise is to let him go

Just a little bit of self-control

I was loved but despised

Guess the feelings were disguised

This sour feeling I detest

Clutching deep in my chest

Heartaches

I'm sorry for the heartache

Which were mainly for my sake

I hope you'd be able to forsake

All my mistakes

I'm sorry for the damages

That led to your high rage

I'll try not to be selfish

And be a girl you'd always cherish

I'm sorry for breaking your heart

And tearing us apart

Mirror on the Wall

Mirror on the wall

Who am I really?

Hoping you could show me

For I feel this face is fake

Disguised smiles stays still

Like my face was made of steel

So I'm hoping you could show me

My true reflection

Lyric of My Heart

Can you hear the lyrics of my song?

The message from my gong

To ease the wrong

I have done

Listen gently to the lyrics of my song

The message from my gong

The promises I hope not to prolong

To show you to whom you belong

Listen again to the soothe g song

From the lips of the throng

Reassuring to keep you all yearlong

Again It's Raining

Again it's raining

Again I'm happy

Again I'm racing

To be in the rain

In the rain

I feel safe

With hands stretched out

And tongue tucked out.

Let the rain purify me

As white as snow again

Let the rain cleanse me

Of all my stain

Again it's raining

Again I'm happy

Let me drown in this ecstasy

In the smell of earth after rain.

I'm Like That Shadow

I am like that shadow

Unseen and unwanted

I am forced to linger

I'm voiceless and faceless

My pleads aren't heard

And my sorrows are not felt

I am only but a reflection

He Died

Aged with sorrow

Burdened with grieve

Dines with depression

And contemplates suicide

He's drowning

Silently breaking

He's yelling

Silently reaching out

He's begging

Silently pleading

He's dying

Silently fading

He's fed up

.........he died

A Friend to the Dark

The dark calls me

I guess I'm part of it

I am known there

So I must be approached

The dark wants me

My soul's as dark as coal

And my life as dirty as dirt

The dark beckons to me

Because it has found in me

A faithful friend

Features of My Man

His eyes shines as the sun

His nose alluring like a rose

His lips, perfectly curved as the moon

These are features of the man

Who holds my heart and soul

He is a lamplight in the dark

A ray of sunshine

And a fountain to drink from

These are the qualities of the man

Who holds my heart and soul

Void of Emotions

I am void of emotions

Drained, I lay hanging

Waiting to catch a glimpse of light

And courage to move on

I am void of emotions

My eyes betrays that fact

My lips in a thin line

I am void of emotions

Drained and empty

I lay waiting

For hope to walk in

Dear Conscience

Dear conscience

I know you've always been around

Like a shadow, you linger

Halting my subconscious

Dear conscience

An anchor for my soul

In the silence you speak

A voice so voiceless

Revealing your humanity

She's The Maiden

She's the maiden

With aching shoulders

She's that lonely flower

Beautiful but sacred

She blossoms alone

Her wails lingers

Like dirge, it's sad

A broken piece

None can fix

She's the maiden

Whose poem you read now

Adultery

Don't tell him I laid with you

The thought of it makes me ewe

The stains, it lingers like taboo

The scars of a taboo.

Don't tell him I laid with you

That's going to break him a part

Our vows lays broken

The guilt rips me

Clutching my soul

Scars

I have a lot of scars

Which I'm not proud of

But as days rolls into weeks

And weeks into months

Months into years

I glance down at those scars

With a deep hole in my heart

As I reminisce on the memories

Behind each scar

Bride's Joy

Oh what great joy and pride

Of becoming a bride

And the thought of the awaiting bliss

Of a sweetened kiss

And the joy of the awaiting night

Makes me swell in delight

And then I dwell in pleasure

Which I cannot measure

And when I recall the past

And the praise

For living in virtuous ways

Though in hardship I was raised

I thrived to follow the right paths

So on this awaiting night

I would lay in the arms of my man

And I hope to be lost in the love

Of this beautiful wedding night

On This Quiet Night

On this quiet night

With the raging wind

And comforting drops of rain

Silently i ponder on you

On this quiet night

I've found solace in the dark again

With its arms wrapped around me

And you running through my mind

Bliss

The night was lovely

But he was so lonely

And towards her room he headed slowly

He stepped in quietly

Found her sleeping soundly

He laid next to her anxiously

Heard her breathing softly

He caressed her gently

She opened her eyes slowly

And he kissed her eagerly

She responded quickly

They made love silently

Moaning and gasping quietly

Until he slipped out the night of bliss

With a sweet kiss

Selfless Love

For you I had nothing

In you I found something

That meant everything

And now I need not to worry about anything

In your weakness I'll stand firm

Speaking words of strength to reaffirm

And I'll keep chasing this love I yearn

Hoping your heart to earn

I'd do anything for you

I'd lose all to be yours

I'd give all for a lifetime with you

To you I confess my selfless love

To you I render my broken heart

To be safe in your heart

Virginity

I said I'd keep it

Till that night I'll wait

They thought I wasn't alright

"Mary the second" they jeered

I was mocked for what's right

But from fornication, I hope to abstain

And my dreams to attain

I'll keep my stance

Forgetting lustful advances

And I pray to uphold this image

With great courage

The Night

I look forward to the night

When peace interrupts

Filling me up

Overflowing

Though lonely as it may be

With no life than i

Still I look forward to the night

I look forward to the night

With aching shoulder laid

Floating on the lullabies

Of the creeping insects

Though dark as black

Without the moon

Still I look forward to the night

My Uncleanliness

I may look churchy

And dress scantly

I may be a beauty

And sound chatty and flirty

But I am faulty

And actually guilty

For sins so plenty

For my heart is dirty

And my soul filthy

I Miss

I miss our sex

And how your hands fills my neck

I miss the flirty words you say

And how it brightens my day

I miss the fire in me you ignite

Leaving me moaning all through the night

Crying Without Tears

When I recall the past

I doubt this love will last

Now I want our love anew

And that love I hope to pursue

But you left without a clue

They say action speaks louder

But I guess your eyes speaks loudest

At times I steal a glance

At you

Hoping for a chance

To say how much I love you

.........im crying without tears

I Am Sour

I am sour

Sour to love, sour to feel

Sour to see

What's right in front of me

I am sour

Sour to give, sour to take

A step further to me

Is a step to a bitter life

I am, sour

Sour to taste, sour to own

A step further to me

Is a step to a broken heart

The Dark Consoles Me

The dark consoles me

With its shouting silence

A voiceless tune I understand

One that reflects me

The dark absorbs my wails

With its cuddles, so comforting

I long to feel

The dark is a faithful friend

Conscious of my hidden desires

Blending to its black darkness

I remain unseen

Oh I Wish I Had Him

Oh how I wish I could have his arms around me,

To caress my blossom with intense tenderness,

His fingertips drawing lines on my skin,

Leaving me burning for more

Oh how I wish I could touch him

To lay my hands slowly on him

Steadily moving to explore

Leaving me in gasps and admiration

Oh how I wish I could hear his husky voice

Whispering to me how much he had missed me

With warm hands trailing down my body

Leaving me shivering at his tender touch.

Oh how I wish to lay underneath him

Watching his eyes burning with desire

With parted lips awaiting his

And breaths caught in my throat

Oh how I wish to have him

Body, mind, and soul

To fill this void of loneliness

With a night of intimacy

And his moans, a beautiful tune

Leaving me breathless till dawn

Oh how I wish I had his arms around me

To keep me warm forever

Exhausted

Knuckle Buckle

Shackle Startle

Tumble Grumble

Hustle Battle

Heartache Headache

Runaway Go away

Forward Backward

Exhausted Abducted

Rest again, Pain again

The Sun is Cruel

The sun is so cruel

It makes my skin cry

A piercing groan that seeks shelter

It burn

Could rain wash the pain away?

Soothing the burn

With its heavy drops dancing on me

Locked In

I wish I was free

To break this shell and flee

Like the bee id run

Towards the light that shines afar

I wish I was free

To break this shell and flee

Id dance around the moon

Telling her of the old me

Distant as the stars

My dreams lay

My minds held me captive

I'm being locked in

I wish I was free

To break this shell and flee

Homeless

He's lain there

Cold as ice

Even as the wind whispered

About his unclothed body

He's lain bare

Homeless but a bridge's paradise

With little food catered

And a care from nobody

In the rain

He's drained

In the sun

He's burned

Homeless but a bridge's paradise

If we be a little selfless

We'd be able to lend a helping hand

To those homeless

As they regain their stand

A Message

I wanna pass a massage

To the one behind my found knowledge

The love you encouraged

Was all damaged

Cause I'm a savage

Perhaps I was being selfish

The love wasn't nourished

So it didn't flourish

I let it perish

A distance, I kept

The withdrawal you felt

Though it wasn't a mistake

Hope you'd forsake

I wasn't fake either

Just didn't come closer

I'm not a player

But I'm not better

....one heart torn apart

I'm sorry

My Guilt

Starring at my phone

Thinking I'm so prone

To be addicted to porn

I know its filth

Yet I watch with guilt

I know it's vain

Yet I watch with pain

I'm in need of a helper

One id always run to

Entranced

Nkem

You've been my anchor

Cuddled by your calmness

You leave me breathless

I fell into your arms

So strong…. So strong they caught me

Hot as furnace

You leave me burning for you

Your heart sang odes

My soul danced to its tunes

So let's make this a sonnet

As we await sunset

And as long as the night bares us witness

Our love shall never weaken

The Truth

The truth is masked

And thereby surpassed

But the truth is what sets us free

Yet we are so blinded to see

The answer just in blurs

We plead for peace

But we forsake love

Like caged birds we long to be free

But as lions they roar back at us

Songs of sorrow now sang

For the dead who died dreadfully

We long for a change

But change mocks us with her silence

Sad Night

The moon is sad tonight

But the trees are dancing cheeringly

Although the street's not booming like the fortnight

Sweet music is playing merrily

The moon is sad tonight

Reflecting my plight

Thus darkness calls me quietly

And all I do is drift silently

Loner

The real me is hidden

To fit in

I rein in my pain

A hurt I can't detain

I forsake my heartaches

To partake in the worlds flake

I'm lain apart

But none can my heart

Underneath those smiles I wear

Lies the fear

I'm a loner

With no other

Single Yet a Parent

Single yet a parent

A mother of two

A father too

A burden so transparent

Single yet a parent

An ordeal to embrace with complaint

A responsibility to shoulder

Without murmurs nor anger

My Love for You

My love for you

Is deeper than the sea

Refreshing like dew

And as beautiful as any butterfly may be

My love for you

Bares no scar

My feelings are true

It has no mar

Writer's Block

Damn this writer's block

It's gotten my mind padlocked

Many words I've tried to unlock

Even the tick tock from the clicking clock

Can't bring me a little luck

And when I think I've gotten a word

I find it absurd

As blank as my paper

As cold as ice

My mind remains

Love in Disguise

He came into my heart

But didn't last

We dated for a while

But it wasn't worth the while

He took my heart in his

But was broken to pieces

My love to him I gave

But was dumped in a grave

I was being staved

For the love I craved

I thought my love was received

Rather I was being deceived

He came to take

Putting all in a fake

I'm all alone

It was a lie all along

In a fool's paradise I reigned

Waiting for love to attain

I pray karma

Gives you a taste

Of your actions

......but love why are you so mean to me

What If

What if the world was just plain?

And they are no pain

Would we really hurt so much?

Would we really cry this much?

What if we were in Eden?

Would all these pain be needed?

That fruit she hadn't eaten

Would we still thrive to be breathing?

Would we have felt this heartache?

That keeps us awake

A pain we can't shake off

So we rather lay off

But what if we really did sin

Yet he didn't come to pay the price

Guess we would have suffered this twice

And we would have paid the sacrifice

With our dear lives

Be My Poet

Be my poet

And I your poetess

Fill my mouth with the lyrics of thy heart

Let thy words slide through me

Touching every part of me

Let thy hands caress my soul

For in it lies my vulnerability

Be my poet

And I your poetess

Holding unto me

As we pour our minds out on paper

Woo me gently

Showing me reasons to keep up

Light up candles for a romantic scene

As I in turn give you an erotic scene

With this mantle in our hands

Be my poet

And I your poetess

Let's lay side by side

Speaking tender words of wisdom

To soothe our ears

Turn me on

Let your hands arouse me

Dive into me

Getting to the center of my poetic soul

Let's ride all night on poetry

As we both hit orgasm

Watch my body dance to the rhythm of your hands

Touch me with every verse

And watch me respond in reverse

Watch me moan words of chant

As I in turn give you an ode

Be my poet

And I your poetess

Riding all night on poetry

As we dwell in the twilight

Of this beautiful night